Christmas 2020
Brother Ryan,
May this tale to ever-more Betterment, Love & Self Mastery.

Marc Gasol: The Inspiring Story of One of Basketball's Most Dominant Centers

An Unauthorized Biography

I look forward to continuing to grow & foster success in our family as Brothers!

By: Clayton Geoffreys

Copyright © 2016 by Calvintir Books, LLC

All rights reserved. Neither this book nor any portion thereof may be reproduced or used in any manner whatsoever without the express written permission. Published in the United States of America.

Disclaimer: The following book is for entertainment and informational purposes only. The information presented is without contract or any type of guarantee assurance. While every caution has been taken to provide accurate and current information, it is solely the reader's responsibility to check all information contained in this article before relying upon it. Neither the author nor publisher can be held accountable for any errors or omissions.

Under no circumstances will any legal responsibility or blame be held against the author or publisher for any reparation, damages, or monetary loss due to the information presented, either directly or indirectly. This book is not intended as legal or medical advice. If any such specialized advice is needed, seek a qualified individual for help.

Trademarks are used without permission. Use of the trademark is not authorized by, associated with, or sponsored by the trademark owners. All trademarks and brands used within this book are used with no intent to infringe on the trademark owners and only used for clarifying purposes.

This book is not sponsored by or affiliated with the National Basketball Association, its teams, the players, or anyone involved with them.

Visit my website at www.claytongeoffreys.com
Cover photo by Verse Photography is licensed under CC BY 2.0 / modified from original

Table of Contents

Foreword 1

Introduction 4

Chapter 1: Early Life and Childhood 10

Chapter 2: High School Career 14

Chapter 3: Marc Gasol's Professional Career in Spain 22

Chapter 4: Marc Gasol's NBA Career 28

    Getting Drafted 28

    Rookie Season 33

    Second Year 37

    The Anchor of the Grit-and-Grind Eras 41

    All-Star Season 55

    Defensive Player of the Year Winner 63

    Injury Plagued Season and New Coach 77

    Return to All-Star Form and Becoming One of the NBA's Best Centers 85

Chapter 5: Marc Gasol's Personal Life 97

Chapter 6: Marc Gasol's Legacy and Future 99

Final Word/About the Author 105

Foreword

Marc Gasol has made an impressionable impact on the Memphis Grizzlies franchise, following in the footsteps of his older brother Pau in leading the Grizzlies beginning in the later part of the first decade of the new millennium. Since entering the league, Gasol has established himself as one of the elite centers to play the game today with an ability to post up in the paint or to take a quick midrange shot. His versatility is similar to his brother in that he adopted many popular European elements to his game, which has helped him remain quite healthy relative to peers who are limited by their shooting range to scoring only inside the paint. Thank you for purchasing *Marc Gasol: The Inspiring Story of One of Basketball's Most Dominant Centers*. In this unauthorized biography, we will learn Marc Gasol's incredible life story and impact on the game of basketball. Hope you enjoy and if you do, please do not forget to leave a review!

Also, check out my website at claytongeoffreys.com to join my exclusive list where I let you know about my latest books. To thank you for your purchase, you can go to my site to download a free copy of *33 Life Lessons: Success Principles, Career Advice & Habits of Successful People*. In the book, you'll learn from some of the greatest thought leaders of different industries on what it takes to become successful and how to live a great life.

Cheers,

Clayton Geoffreys

Visit me at www.claytongeoffreys.com

33 LIFE LESSONS

SUCCESS PRINCIPLES, CAREER ADVICE
& HABITS OF SUCCESSFUL PEOPLE

CLAYTON GEOFFREYS

Introduction

As the sport of basketball has grown over the years, not only in the United States, but in all other parts of the globe as well, the NBA has seen a flurry of European super-stars crossing over from the shores of Europe to play professional basketball in the world's best basketball league. Despite many international basketball players coming over to the NBA since the 90's, it was only in the new millennium when the NBA truly became global. The 90's saw its share of very good European players such as Toni Kukoc, Vlade Divac, Rik Smits, Arvydas Sabonis, and the late, great Drazen Petrovic. Coincidentally, a lot of those international players come from European nations because of how fundamentally sound their players are.

The new millennium saw an even bigger explosion of European talent joining several NBA teams. Notable European players that became popular NBA stars in the new decade include Dirk Nowitzki, Tony Parker,

Andrei Kirilenko, Peja Stojakovic, and Luis Scola, among others. However, one European basketball star literally stands taller than others. That man is Marc Gasol.

If you go back six to eight years ago, you would immediately think of Pau Gasol whenever you hear the "Gasol" family name. After all, Pau was the European superstar who put Spain on the map as arguably the second best basketball country in the world. Pau also had won championships with the Lakers in the late 2000s. He was the Spanish basketball team's best player and could very well be Spain's best in their basketball history. Hence, Pau was essentially a household name among basketball fans and was considered one of the best big men in all of basketball.

Over the years, Pau's younger brother Marc slowly and steadily worked his way up to becoming one of today's best NBA players. Standing 7'1" and weighing nearly 270 lbs., Marc was larger than his big brother. When he entered the NBA in 2008, people thought that size was the only thing that Marc had over Pau. Pau was one of the league's best and most fundamentally sound big men while Marc was just a giant who would live in the shadow of his big brother. He was just a second round draft pick while Pau was a top prospect in his draft class.

Fast forward to the present-day NBA and you would be shocked to see Marc's name at the top of the list with some of the league's best centers. Marc Gasol has become a two-time All-Star, a Defensive Player of the Year, an All-NBA First and Second Team member, an All-Defensive Second Team member, and a two-time Olympic silver medalist. He has flooded his resume with a lot of achievements and awards since coming to the NBA. He has become as good as his brother Pau, and it could even be argued to be the better of the Gasol brothers right now. He currently has a career average of 14.1 points, 7.9 rebounds, 3 assists, and 1.6 blocks. Not bad for a second round pick.

Today, Marc Gasol has been recognized as one of the league's best centers. Aside from being a giant, Marc is as skillful as any other big man in the league, not just on offense but on defense as well. On defense, he shadows the paint and is great at rotating defensive assignments. He is the Grizzlies' defensive anchor and vocal leader. Marc is also considered one of the top passing NBA centers. His passing skills rival those of point guards, and is second only to Mike Conley on the Grizzlies' roster. In the post, he is a serious threat because he can bully smaller players for baskets or get around slower centers with his superior footwork. When ganged-up on in the paint, Marc can easily make plays for his teammates. Pushing him out of the paint has never been an option either, because he can shoot perimeter jumpers or see over the top of the defense for easy passes for cutters. With Marc's array of skills on any spot on the floor, there's no reason why he should not be considered as the top center in the league.

Aside from being considered as a great center in the NBA, Marc Gasol has also become the Memphis Grizzlies' best player and franchise star. He is the perfect player for Memphis' grind-it-out or grind-and-grind style of slowing down the game pace and playing physical defense. He is simply the personification of the Grizzlies' style of basketball as he is the anchor on both offense and defense.

Despite Memphis' very physical style, Marc Gasol is considered to be a gentle giant both on and off the court. On the basketball court, he moves with grace and has the same kind of gentle footwork Pau has always had. Off the court, Marc and his brother are known philanthropists. They run the Gasol Foundation, which aims to improve the health and lifestyle of today's youth through sports, proper nutrition, and mental counseling. Marc has a special place in his heart for this this foundation because he was once an overweight kid. Marc is also a known ambassador of the St. Jude Children's Research Hospital in both Spain and the USA.[i]

Together with his brother Pau, Marc Gasol has transformed Spain into a basketball powerhouse and is arguably the second best basketball nation next to the United States of America. Since joining the Spanish basketball team in 2006, he and Pau have formed the most dominant frontline in international basketball today as the pair of 7-footers consistently dominates every other frontline in FIBA and in the Olympics. His domination in the international realm has earned Spain two silver medals in the Olympics and a gold medal in the FIBA World Championships.

With Marc Gasol's achievements in the NBA, the international basketball realm, and in the more important field of philanthropy and service to humanity, it is not far-off to say that Marc also figuratively stands taller than all other European basketball players in NBA history.

Chapter 1: Early Life and Childhood

Marc Gasol Saez is of Spanish descent born on January 29, 1985 and raised in Barcelona, Spain. He was born to parents Augusti Gasol and Marisa Saez. Augusti worked as a hospital administrator in Spain while Marisa was a doctor working in the same hospital. It was there, in the hospital, where his parents met. Aside from working in the same hospital, both Gasol parents played the same sport, basketball, which all their children would soon play.

Marc has two other brothers, both of whom play basketball. His older brother Pau is also a professional basketball player in the NBA. Pau, who stands 7-feet tall, is a multiple-time All-Star and has played for the Memphis Grizzlies, the Los Angeles Lakers (where he won two NBA championships), and currently plays for the Chicago Bulls. Pau is almost five years older than Marc, and his younger brother Adria is about eight years younger than him. Adria is a basketball player who used to play for the University of California at Los Angeles (UCLA) Bruins but has since returned to Spain to play professional basketball there after not being able to play a single minute with the Bruins.[ii] Adria is slightly shorter than both of his brothers standing at 6'10" and the build of his body more closely resembles his eldest brother than Marc. With all three Gasol brothers standing more or less 7-feet tall, we can conclude that the Gasol parents have good genetics.

With Pau being greatly interested in the game of basketball because of the Dream Team in the 1992 Barcelona Olympics, Marc followed suit with his brother. Marc joined Barcelona's Youth Basketball Club where he would get his first crack at playing organized basketball.[iii] It was also there that Marc learned the fundamentals of playing basketball. Since he was comparatively taller than most of the kids in his age group, Marc always played the big man position, even during his childhood.

Pau became a teenage basketball star in Europe and the NBA began to keep its eye on the eldest Gasol brother. With Pau making his way to the NBA via the 2001 NBA Draft, the Gasol family had to relocate to the United States, specifically to Memphis, Tennessee where Pau was drafted. Marc transferred from Spain to Lausanne Collegiate School, a private school in east Memphis, at barely 16 years old. When Marc learned of the news, he was playing with the Spanish Under-16 Basketball Team in France.

Augusti and Marisa both quit their jobs so that they could help their sons adjust to living in a whole new and entirely different environment. Pau thought that such a gesture was a testament to how close-knit their family was. The Gasol family rented an apartment in Memphis. There were merely three bedrooms. Marc had to share a room with Adria, which was kind of awkward considering how big the Gasol brothers were.[iv]

Though Barcelona isn't a small city, Marc was first shocked about how wide and free Memphis looked. It was not as populated as his hometown and everything in the city was huge, including the streets, the cars, and the buildings. However, the biggest shock to Marc Gasol at the time was that he had to leave his team FC Barcelona, where he felt the most comfort during his time in Spain.[v]

Chapter 2: High School Career

When the Gasol family relocated to Memphis, Marc initially enrolled at White Station. However, White Station was too big of a school for Marc Gasol who was just trying to immerse himself in living in the United States. Hence, he transferred to Lausanne, which was smaller and had a lot of international students.

Marc Gasol immediately played for the varsity team in Lausanne. Back then, Marc barely knew how to speak English and knew nothing about American culture or their style of playing basketball. The only English he could mutter on his first day was, "I am Marc. I play basketball. I am from Barcelona." Marc had to learn a lot about American culture, particularly that of Tennessee's. He had acquainted himself with the music of Elvis Presley and of Memphis hip-hop during the first two years that he would spend in Memphis. It was also lucky for him that Lausanne was a hub for international students who could speak Spanish. Having Spanish-speaking friends helped the young Gasol learn the English language.[vi]

Basketball was how Marc communicated because it was, in his own words, an "international language." He rarely spoke with the people around and would express himself through simple gestures. Though he would rarely talk, everybody in the campus loved the gentle giant because of his happy and cheerful demeanor. Marc always had a smile on his face, even on the basketball court.[vii]

Everybody in Memphis knew about Pau Gasol, but Marc was simply known as the younger brother of Pau. Back when he first transferred to Lausanne, he was almost 7-feet tall and was taller than his age group. The next tallest was merely 6'4". Marc was not only a tall 6'10" teenager, he was literally a huge kid who weighed more than 300 lbs. at his heaviest in high school, unlike his brother Pau who was lean and fit.[viii] Marc could not even fit within the 250 lbs. weight limit of the Lausanne scales. In the words of his high school assistant coach Jon Van Hoozer, Marc was a "massive human being," even as a high school boy. Even his teachers would often laugh at the memory of Marc hitting his head when entering classrooms. Even Dirk Nowitzki, who saw Marc during the 2002 All-Star Weekend when Pau was participating in the rookie game, was shocked at how huge Marc was. With his unusual size, Marc was nicknamed "The Big Burrito" because of his chubby cheeks.

In his time in Memphis, Marc had a deep love for McDonald's staple burger, the Big Mac. His former teammate Karon Nash would recount that Marc's appetite was so big that he would always order two or more Big Macs. Fast food was something new to him, and his diet suffered because of it. As Marc would later admit, being young and dumb was how he picked up those bad habits, but has used those memories of his fat self as a motivation to be a better-conditioned player.

Marc Gasol was simply unstoppable in high school. Marc did have a set of refined skills he picked up in Spain. However, his skills could not see the light of day because he would just overpower his opposition for points and rebounds. As Shane Battier, who played for the Grizzlies when Marc was in high school, would point out, "Marc was 'like King Kong' on the basketball court." Despite his dominance on the court, what shocked everyone was that he was unselfish. Everyone knew he could score all the points if he wanted to, but he was playing semi-point guard with how he wanted to involve everyone.[ix]

With the arrival of Marc Gasol in Lausanne, high school coach Jason Peters immediately thought that their team would see a revival. Lausanne was neither a basketball school, nor even a sports breeding ground. Their basketball team only mustered to win 10 games from 1993 to 1998.[x] However, the basketball team was also like the United Nations. They had a Serbian point guard by the name of Mladen Mrkaic who grew to be one of Marc's closest friends in Memphis. Prior to his days in Lausanne, Mrkaic was also a youth team member in Europe and had played a few times against Marc. Mrkaic was Lausanne's best player prior to the arrival of Marc. Mrkaic and Gasol made the team relevant. In later months, Lausanne's basketball games became a sensation that the house was always packed with fans.

Despite being arguably the best high school player in Memphis at that time, Marc was still living in the shadow of his brother Pau. Pau was the best player in Memphis and was always a borderline All-Star if not an All-Star. However, Marc was never bothered by that fact. He was dedicated to making his own path. Never did he try to wear his brother's Grizzlies gear, nor did he boast the fact that he was the younger brother of an All-Star NBA player. He was confident with who he was, but was never overconfident, and always carried himself with a low profile on campus.

In Marc Gasol's high school career at Lausanne, he averaged 26 points and 10 rebounds per game. Peters would call him a fat version of Larry Bird because of his passing skills and because he had a pure shot that could extend all the way out to the amateur three-point line. Above everything else, Gasol's unselfishness was what made him stand out. With his size and skillset, he could have dominated the stats sheet, but still chose to make his teammates better.

Marc was so unstoppable in high school that opposing teams would slow the game down to a snail's pace. Since there was no shot clock, opponents would just hold on to the ball for a very long time. As Marc was not familiar to a game without a shot clock, he often yelled at the referees to do something and also often got technical fouls. When they faced Briarcrest Christian School, the opposing team even tried to force Gasol out of the paint using Michael Oher. Oher is now known in football as the offensive tackle for the Baltimore Ravens. Oher was so strong and burly that he could prevent the gigantic Gasol from entering the paint. However, Gasol used his perimeter shooting touch to counterattack Oher.[xi]

In his first season with the team, he almost led them to the state tournament. The following year, Gasol and Lausanne were even better and stronger. He averaged 26 points, 13 rebounds, and 6 assists that year on his way to the state championship game. Lausanne faced Brentwood Academy who had a future NBA player Brendan Wright on their team. Lausanne lost that game but Gasol was named Mr. Basketball that year.

After his senior year, Gasol had a choice to make. His options were to play for US colleges in the NCAA or to go back to Spain. The University of Memphis even recruited him as a walk-on. Ultimately, he chose his hometown because he believed that his size was what would hinder him from improving his game in the NCAA. In his own words, he needed structure and needed to re-learn the basics of basketball. Because Europe is so famous for instilling the fundamental basketball skills into their players, Spain was the best choice for the young Marc Gasol.[xii]

Chapter 3: Marc Gasol's Professional Career in Spain

Marc has always been a part of the FC Barcelona team, even since his early days. It was in 1998 that he joined the FC Barcelona youth team while his brother Pau was playing for the senior team. He stayed in the youth team until 2001 when Pau decided to go to the NBA. Marc would return to FC Barcelona two years later as an oversized teenager.

Back in Spain, Marc played for FC Barcelona in the Liga ACB. There were no more Big Macs for the professional basketball player. Marc Gasol had to improve his diet and conditioning. He improved his physique in Spain because he was so disgusted at how big he already was. As Peters would recount, Marc could barely dunk the ball in high school because he was so heavy. That all changed when Marc learned how to control his diet and how to work on his body.

Marc lived in La Masia back in Spain. La Masia was a popular academy for young soccer and basketball players. It was his stay there that helped him improved on his conditioning. He only ate meals that were served there and rarely ate fast food. Marc also trained and practiced up to three times a day. That was the opportunity he had to reshape his body and transform the pudgy Marc Gasol into a burly mountain of a man.

It was also back in Barcelona where Marc Gasol re-learned the basics of the game. He basically refined and perfected the fundamentals of his basketball game. While colleges in the United States might have exposed him to elite competition and might have taught him advanced tactical decisions on the court, Spain or Europe in general was where any player would go if they wanted to have all the fundamental elements of the game mastered.

In 2003, a year after Marc returned to Spain, the Memphis Grizzlies went to Barcelona for a tune-up game against FC Barcelona. Then Memphis head coach Lionel Hollins was shocked at how much Marc had improved and changed in terms of physique. He recounted how Pau would dominate Marc back in Memphis when they would play one-on-one. Pau was so much better and so much fit than the then chubby Marc. Pau could easily block Marc's shot without so much as lifting his feet off the ground. But in the tune-up game against Marc's FC Barcelona, Marc could already hold his own against his brother.[xiii]

Marc Gasol became a better post player in his five years in Spain. While Marc would retain the consistent shooting touch he always had, he however stopped shooting too much perimeter and outside jumpers and dwelled inside the paint where he could dominate with his size and strength. Gasol would spend three seasons for FC Barcelona but mostly as a reserve center off the bench. He averaged only 1.3 points on barely six minutes of action in his first season. His role and his minutes increased every year. In his second season, he averaged 5 points and almost four rebounds in 16 minutes per game. In the 2005-06 season, his final with FC Barcelona, Marc averaged 4.1 points and 2.2 rebounds in almost 10 minutes per game. Though he still wasn't seeing too much action, he won the Spanish League championship with Barcelona in 2004. Despite Gasol not getting the exposure he would have wanted in Barcelona, he was exposed to something that would mean just as much as any achievement he would gain in his career: romance. It was in Barcelona where Marc met his wife-to-be Cristina Blesa. Cristina was one of the people who pushed Marc on improving his diet and was an inspiration for him to become a more confident basketball player. To date, Marc still credits Cristina for how much better he has become.[xiv]

In 2006, just in time for the FIBA World Championship, Marc suited up for the Spanish basketball team for the first time in his life. In a reserve role for the national team, Marc averaged 5.5 points and 3.2 rebounds to help Spain win the gold medal in Japan. Marc's impressive performance in the tournament earned him the attention of another ACB team, Akasvayu Girona. He signed with Akasvayu Girona and saw his minutes and his role jumping. From being a benchwarmer in Barcelona, he suddenly became the starting center for Girona. In his first season in his new team, Marc averaged 10.8 points and 5.5 rebounds as the focal point for the inside offense of Girona, a role he was not so accustomed to after spending most of his time on the bench with FC Barcelona.

Prior to the 2007-08 ACB season, the Los Angeles Lakers drafted Marc in the NBA as the 48th overall pick. He dropped in the draft further than he expected. After all, Marc did not have sufficient experience yet due to sitting three years on the FC Barcelona bench. His draft night came right after showing improvement with Akasvayu Girona. Despite the improvement, Marc Gasol was still unproven and untested as a go-to-guy and as a center in the big leagues. The Lakers chose not to buy out Marc's contract with Girona.

Hence, Marc had to stay for one more year in Spain and in his Girona team to further hone his talents.

The following 2007-08 season, Marc Gasol greatly improved and averaged 16.2 points and 8.3 rebounds. He was the offensive focal point of Girona and led the team in scoring and rebounding. In what would he his final season in Spain, Marc Gasol won the Spanish League Most Valuable Player award. In 2008, he became the best player on Spanish shores. It was then that he felt he was ready to go back to the United States to suit up for the Memphis Grizzlies, his brother Pau's former team. In his five seasons in Spain, Marc Gasol averaged 8.5 points, 4.6 rebounds, 1.1 assists, and 1 block. In the same span, he won a title with FC Barcelona and became the league's MVP in 2008 while playing for Akasvayu Girona.

Chapter 4: Marc Gasol's NBA Career

Getting Drafted

Though Marc only started playing in the NBA in the 2008-09 season, he did apply for the NBA Draft in 2007. Back then, he was super raw and had only played sparingly with FC Barcelona for three seasons and in an improved, yet unproven, role with Akasvayu Girona in his fourth season in Spain. Hence, scouts evaluated Marc Gasol based solely on his then mediocre career in Spain a year prior to his breakout MVP season with Akasvayu Girona.

Coming into the 2007 NBA Draft, Marc stood a towering 7'1". In his four seasons as a professional in Spain, he had shed all of his high school weight and improved to 265 lbs. from being over 300 lbs. He was almost unrecognizable from the fat kid playing in the high school gyms in Memphis. Marc Gasol was now a bearded burly mountain of a man. However impressive a man Gasol was in terms of physical stature, he was not one of the best 30 players of the draft class, let alone even a lottery pick. He was still too raw and unrealized.

Though he was not one of the best prospects, Marc Gasol was still one of the more impressive post-up players. He was scouted to be good at finding his position down at the low block and was adept at post fundamentals. Similar to Pau, Marc has always had good soft hands that could easily catch the ball at the post, and he could see over the double team to pass out to open teammates. Unlike his older brother, Marc could overpower his defenders, was very physical, and could still finish with grace. He could hit turnaround jumpers and hook shots as well.[xv]

Marc was also always seen as a good shooter for his size and position. His shooting range can go all the way out to the amateur three-point line, and he could wreak havoc out there whenever he would be denied his position at the post. He was also always a good decision-maker on the court whenever he was doubled or denied his position in the paint. He did not rush shots and could always find an open teammate.[xvi]

However, Marc's downsides were seen as overshadowing his supreme post skillset. He was in stark contrast to Pau Gasol in terms of mobility. Marc was as slow as they come. He did not have the footwork or the foot speed of his older brother. His athletic ability was always limited, and it hindered him from finding his way into an NBA team full of superior athletic players because not too many teams can use the services of an ultra-slow and extremely gravitationally challenged player. Also, at the time of the draft, Marc was still seen as a chubby man. Although he had lost a lot of weight since high school, Marc was still not in supreme condition and was still carrying extra weight. Though he was a very skillful player at the post, his post moves seemed like they were in slow motion and defenders could easily double him up before he could put up a shot.[xvii]

On the defensive end, Marc was not spared of criticisms. He was seen as lacking the lateral quickness and foot speed to keep up with opposing players. His lack of foot speed and mobility could hinder him from rotating defensively, especially on pick and roll switches where the opposing ball handler could easily blow by him for an uncontested dunk at the basket. Marc was criticized to be very vertically challenged when jumping and could not block shots that most NBA centers could easily block. Even if he could somehow contest and defend shots, he was thought to be a mediocre rebounder who was poor at boxing out his man despite his supreme size and strength.

Overall, Marc Gasol was scouted to be a capable low-post player and could get inside baskets whenever they were needed. Yet, scouts and most teams were very iffy on Marc's deep lack when it came to the athletic side. Being very slow and limited, Marc was thought to be a defensive liability and could also be a burden on fast-paced offenses. Due to his limitations, Marc was predicted as a second round pick, especially because he was still in a contract with Akasvayu Girona. The team that would draft him would have to buy out his contract with his Spanish team if they wanted his services immediately.

True enough, Marc Gasol was not a top prospect. He was not selected in the top 10 of the 2007 draft, nor was he even chosen in the first round. In the second round, Marc wasn't even in the top 10. The younger Gasol was drafted 18th in the second round and 48th overall in the 2007 NBA Draft. It was the Los Angeles Lakers that wanted to gamble on Marc Gasol. With the team roster already packed with centers such as Kwame Brown, Chris Mihm, Andrew Bynum, and DJ Mbenga, the Lakers did not buy out Gasol's contract with Girona. With that, Marc Gasol stayed in Spain for one more season where he dominated and won the MVP.

On February 1, 2008 and nearly a year after he was drafted, the Los Angeles Lakers traded the draft rights of Marc Gasol along with Kwame Brown, Javaris Criitenton, and Aaron Mckie to the Memphis Grizzlies for no other than Marc's older brother Pau Gasol. It was the first and only time in league history that a player was traded to another team in exchange for his brother. It was also the second time in Marc's lifetime that Pau relocated him to Memphis. With Marc's rights traded to the Grizzlies, he was now set to fill in the gap that his brother had left.

Rookie Season

When Marc Gasol's draft rights were drafted to the Memphis Grizzlies in what was initially thought to be one of the most lopsided trades in NBA history, the people and fans of Memphis were disappointed at how they received a lesser version of Pau Gasol in exchange for the elder brother. After all, Marc was unproven and was merely a second round choice while

Pau was a multiple-time All-Star and had just got back from the NBA Finals in a losing effort against the Celtics. Everyone was in shock because of the trade. Shane Battier could not believe what his former team had done, and even Gregg Popovich of the Spurs said that the trade was "beyond comprehension".[xviii]

However, Marc was nowhere near the scrub that most people thought he was. Marc Gasol was not as good as Pau yet but he was a good young piece to rebuild a team around. Fresh from a silver medal finish in the 2008 Olympic Games in China, Marc was ready to take his size and talents to the NBA. He had a respectable outing in the Olympics, averaging 7.1 points and 4.6 rebounds while starting alongside his brother for the Spanish men's basketball team.

Since Marc spent one more year in Spain after he was drafted, he became a steal for the Memphis Grizzlies when he finally came to the NBA. That extra year in Spain paid dividends for Marc. He became Spain's most dominant player that year. The Olympic experience also helped him get accustomed to how the NBA game is so much different from the competition in Spain. Indeed, the extra year paid off as Memphis GM Chris Wallace believed that Marc Gasol could have been a lottery pick if he had joined the NBA Draft in 2008 instead. He also said that Marc was the player they were after when they made the trade with the Lakers.

When Gasol joined the Grizzlies in 2008, the team had a young and talented core. They had just drafted a proven shooter OJ Mayo for the third overall pick that year. The previous season, they drafted capable point guard Mike Conley Jr. The roster also included a young athletic scorer Rudy Gay at the wing and Hakeem Warrick at the power forward spot. The Grizzlies main hole in the lineup was that they lacked depth at the center position. Their centers were 7-footer Darko Milicic and recently drafted 7'2" Hamed Haddadi who was one of the most dominating players in Asia. With the paint-dweller spot up for grabs, it was easy for Marc Gasol to dominate the majority of the minutes as the center.

Marc Gasol was not the disappointment that many people thought he was. In fact, he had a very respectable start to the season. Marc Gasol went on to score more than 10 points in 10 straight games to start his rookie season. Contrary to what scouts said about him, Marc was actually a very capable rebounder and led the Grizzlies in that department.

Despite the respectable performances of Marc Gasol and the young Grizzlies core, the Grizzlies finished the season with a 24-win and 58-loss record that was at the near bottom of the Western Conference. Obviously, Memphis did not reach the playoffs in the first full season of the post-Pau Gasol era. Marc Gasol had a good year as a rookie. He was selected in the All-Rookie Second Team with averages of 11.9 points, 7.4 rebounds, and 1.1 swats. Marc even broke his brother's field goal percentage for a rookie record by shooting 53% compared to his brother's 52%. Though he did not win Rookie of the Year like his brother, who won the NBA title in Marc's rookie season, and though his numbers were not as gaudy as Pau's, there was no doubt that Marc belonged in the NBA and would soon become one of its best centers.

Second Year

Marc Gasol was ready to further improve his game for the young Memphis Grizzlies team. Mark was fresh from a gold medal victory for Spain in the 2009 FIBA Euro Championship and was one of the best players on that Spanish team. However, he was not content with becoming one of Spain's best players because he wanted to be one of the best players on the Grizzlies roster in the 2009-10 NBA season.

The Memphis Grizzlies had a promising team of young talent who all had good seasons the previous year. Adding veteran leadership to that core, the Grizzlies signed former superstar Allen Iverson for a one-year deal and also the burly Zach Randolph, who was one of the best power forwards the time, in a trade for Quentin Richardson. They also added another center into the lineup by drafting 7'3" shot blocker Hasheem Thabeet with the 3rd overall pick and DeMarre Carroll with the 27th overall pick in the 2009 Draft. With their offseason acquisitions, it was evident that the Grizzlies wanted to make a run at a playoff spot.

The season did not start as well as the Grizzlies had wanted it to. Allen Iverson would play only the first three games for the Grizzlies before permanently leaving the team due to personal reasons. Despite losing a sure-fire Hall of Fame player and one of the best superstars the NBA has ever seen, the Grizzlies improved their play on the strength of the much-improved Marc Gasol and their new acquisition Zach Randolph who was playing at the best level he has ever played. Gasol and Randolph will soon become the cornerstones of what would become the grit-and-grind Memphis Grizzlies even to this day.

Despite the presence of another big center in the lineup in the form of Thabeet, Marc Gasol's minutes at the center position increased nonetheless. He would play five more minutes than his rookie season, not because the Grizzlies lacked centers, but because Marc Gasol just outplayed every other center in Grizzlies uniform. Hasheem Thabeet did not live up to the hype as the third overall draft pick while Hamed Haddadi did not improve as much as the team wanted him to.

Meanwhile, the Grizzlies were primed to a playoff push with the terrific play of their young core together with their imposing frontcourt players. Mike Conley proved to be a capable point guard while the wing combo of OJ Mayo and Rudy Gay continued to pile up the points. The stellar play of the then All-Star selection Zach Randolph together with the young core led by Marc Gasol pushed the Memphis Grizzlies to a much-improved record of 40 wins and 42 losses. However, they failed to garner a playoff spot and their season ended abruptly.

Despite not making the playoffs, Marc Gasol continued to show the world that the Pau Gasol trade was not as lopsided as everyone thought it was. By the end of the 2009-10 season, Marc's numbers increased across the board and he averaged 14.6 points, 9.3 rebounds, 2.4 assists, 1 steal, and 1.6 blocks on 58.1% shooting from the field while playing almost 36 minutes. His 58% shooting was the fourth highest field goal percentage in the league that season.

With his game bordering All-Star level, Marc Gasol indeed proved that he was not just a throw-in in that trade for his brother. In fact, Marc was one of the main reasons for the Grizzlies' improvement that year. He was the defensive anchor of the team and he protected the paint well. Once again, Marc proved his doubters wrong. From being scouted as a defensive liability due to his limited mobility, Marc became one of the best paint defenders in the whole NBA. And though he was scouted as a "mediocre rebounder," Marc was second only to Randolph in the team in rebounding. It was

Marc Gasol's presence in the paint that would be the key to how the Grizzlies would now play their daunted grit-and-grind defense, which terrorizes even the best NBA offenses to this date.

The Anchor of the Grit-and-Grind Eras

With how impressive the Grizzlies were last season whenever they would slow the pace down and bank on their defense to win games, Coach Lionel Hollins employed a slow-paced offensive style that focused on the strength of their inside game and on physical pressure defense which led to many turnovers for the opposing team. This kind of a style was beneficial to the slow yet physical big men of the Grizzlies, especially to Marc Gasol, because it played right to their strengths.

Coincidentally, the new grit-and-grind era started in the tenth season of Grizzlies basketball in Memphis. It had been 10 years since the franchise relocated from Vancouver to Memphis and 10 years since they drafted

Pau Gasol. After 10 years, they still had a Gasol that would be their anchor and franchise player. To start off this new era of Grizzlies basketball, the team signed Tony Allen to a three-year deal worth almost $10 million. Tony Allen, who won a title in 2008, was just fresh off a losing effort in the NBA finals against a Lakers team that contained Pau. His veteran leadership and championship experience would prove to be valuable to the Memphis Grizzlies, even to this day. Rudy Gay was also extended an $82 million contract for the next five years. They also drafted big shooting guard Xavier Henry who they thought could provide a lot of scoring and athleticism at the wing spot.

The slow-paced style of the Grizzlies was what they needed in order to become more successful. The presence of Marc Gasol in the paint helped their defense greatly and forced their opponents to under 100 points by average. Because of the physical style of play that the Grizzlies employed especially when playing at home, the FedEx Forum (the Grizzlies' arena) would soon be called The Grindhouse. Hollins started to employ defense-oriented players more and more, especially on the perimeter to pressure the ball. And with OJ Mayo's lack on the defensive end, Hollins relegated him over to the bench and Mayo's production dipped. He preferred starting Tony Allen and Sam Young because of their defensive capabilities. Marc Gasol saw his production dropping that season not only because of the slower style of play but also because of the drop in his minutes. Though Marc Gasol still dominated the minutes at the center position, Lionel Hollins would sometimes employ a smaller lineup by putting Zach Randolph at the center position, and Darrell Arthur and Gay at the forward positions. Though the Grizzlies lost a lot of size and defense with that lineup, they were able to play at a faster pace whenever they needed it. Due to the change of style and the drop in minutes, Marc Gasol only averaged 11.7 points, 7 rebounds, and 1.7 blocks per game. Zach Randolph and Rudy Gay scored the majority of the points for the Grizzlies but Marc was undoubtedly the defensive anchor in the paint.

In the middle of the season, the Grizzlies traded former third overall pick Hasheem Thabeet and DeMarre Carroll over to the Houston Rockets in exchange for Shane Battier and Ish Smith. Thabeet was a great disappointment, not only to the Grizzlies but also to the whole NBA. Thabeet was expected to be the next Dikembe Mutomb and people thought that the Grizzlies would have had one of the most imposing frontlines with Thabeet and Marc in the paint. It never came to fruition though, and Thabeet could barely muster to play 10 minutes a game. The trade was what the Grizzlies needed because they had a lack of defensive depth at the small forward position. Shane Battier filled that need and also provided leadership and experience for the team.

The trade for Battier would prove to be beneficial for the team because they would lose the services of Rudy Gay more than a month after the trade. Gay, the team's second leading scorer, had to undergo left shoulder surgery. Rudy Gay was playing at a career-defining level that season. It was a good thing for the Grizzlies that Battier was there to fill-in the gap at the small forward position after they had lost Gay.

At the end of the season, the Grizzlies were the league's highest scoring team inside the paint because of Zach Randolph and Marc Gasol. The team also had the most steals among all the NBA teams primarily because the grit-and-grind style was beneficial for their perimeter players like Mike Conley and Tony Allen who specialize in pressuring the ball handler to force steals or turnovers. With their new style of play, the Memphis Grizzlies finished the season as the eighth seed in the Western Conference with a 46-win and 36-loss record. It was the first time since 2006 that the Grizzlies would make the playoffs. Despite making the playoffs three other times in the past, the franchise has never won a single playoff game prior to the 2011 playoffs.

The Grizzlies were out to face the top-seeded San Antonio Spurs in the first round of the playoffs. The Spurs were a rejuvenated team that saw an increase in success because of their ball movement. They were led by the Spurs franchise's legendary trio of Tony Parker, Manu Ginobili, and the great Tim Duncan. The Spurs also saw significant contributions from the likes of Richard Jefferson, George Hill, Gary Neal, and Dejuan Blair. Of course, they also had Gregg Popovich who is one of the greatest coaches in NBA history. It was clear and obvious that the Grizzlies lacked the playoff and veteran experience that the Spurs had and it was expected for them to lose quickly to the powerful San Antonio Spurs.

What transpired in the first game was severely unexpected for any basketball fan in the world. The Memphis Grizzlies defeated the San Antonio Spurs in game one with a 101-98 victory. The Grizzlies rode the terrific play of Zach Randolph throughout the game and employed the same kind of pressure defense that disrupted the ball movement offense of the Spurs. Marc Gasol also played good defense on Tim Duncan the whole game. With their game one win, the Grizzlies stole home court advantage from the Spurs and they also recorded the franchise's first ever playoff victory.

Marc Gasol would dominate the rebounds for the Grizzlies in the second game with 17 boards. However, the Spurs rebounded from their loss and defeated the Grizzlies in a close game on the strength of a balanced effort from all their players. Sam Young led the Grizzlies with 17 points and Ginobili led the Spurs with an additional 17 points. With San Antonio winning game two, people began to think that the game one victory was merely a fluke.

Lightning struck twice for the Memphis Grizzlies. They again won against the Spurs in game three when the series shifted over to Memphis and The Grindhouse. The Grizzlies once again rode their three best players, Randolph, Gasol, and Conley, who all played well. Randolph continued to play as if he was the best power forward in the league by scoring 25 points. Gasol grabbed nine boards and Conley delivered 10 dimes. Again, it was a tight victory with only a three-point margin. It was the Memphis defense that got the job down by limiting San Antonio to only 88 points.

The Grindhouse continued to rock in game four. This time, the Grizzlies gave the Spurs a run at their money by winning in a blowout fashion. They defeated the Spurs 105 to 86. Once again, the Grizzlies' defense held the Spurs to under 90 points and it seemed as if the Spurs could not buy a basket against the solid defense of Marc Gasol in the paint. Gasol and Randolph each had nine boards while Conley led the team in points and assists with 17 and seven respectively. The Grizzlies were now up three wins to one and they were only one win away from an upset of epic proportions.

Banking on their veteran and championship experiences, the Spurs managed to stay away from elimination with a 110 to 103 victory in game five after Gary Neal sank a three-pointer to force the game into overtime. The two Memphis behemoths Gasol and Randolph played fantastically again with 17 rebounds and 26 points respectively. It was ultimately the amazing performance by Manu Ginobili that did the Grizzlies in. Manu scored 33 points while playing an unusual role as a starter for the Spurs. Duncan only managed to score 13 points against the defense of Marc Gasol while Tony Parker scored 24.

That game five victory was all the Spurs had left in the series, because the Grizzlies would end their championship aspirations with a 99 to 91 win back in Memphis. The Grizzlies once again banked on Gasol's defense and rebounding but more so on the amazing series performance by Zach Randolph, who had 31 points and 11 rebounds. With the series over, the Grizzlies were finally able to win their first ever playoff series. It was also only the fourth time in NBA history that an eighth seed defeated a first seed in the playoffs. And ever since the playoff format went into a seven-game series for all rounds, it was only the second time that an eighth seed beat the first seed in a seven-game series. The upset was complete and the Grizzlies went rolling into the second round brimming with confidence.

The Memphis Grizzlies went on to face the Oklahoma City Thunder led by an ultra-young and athletic core of the league's leading scorer Kevin Durant, the lightning fast point guard Russell Westbrook, and bench scorer James Harden. The Thunder were the fourth seed in the West, were very hungry, and were just beginning to scratch the surface of their potential.

Once again, the Memphis Grizzlies were up against the odds. Similar to their first round encounter with the Spurs, the Grizzlies upset the OKC Thunder in the first game of the second round with a 114 to 101 victory. Once again, the Grizzlies rode their big frontline with

Zach Randolph scoring a playoff career-high 34 points and with Marc Gasol scoring 20 points and grabbing 13 rebounds. Kevin Durant led the way for the Thunder with 33 points but it was mostly a one-person performance. For the second time in the playoffs, the Memphis Grizzlies stole home court advantage from the higher seeded opponent.

OKC would take revenge for their home loss by winning game two with a 9-point victory. Durant led the way again with 26 points. Randolph's game two performance was a far cry from his previous game with only 15 points. Marc Gasol continued to record double-doubles by scoring 13 points and collecting 10 rebounds. It was Mike Conley who kept them alive with 24 points. When the series shifted to Memphis, the Grizzlies would display their home court dominance by winning an overtime game after trailing by as much as 16 points in the third quarter. The inside presence of Memphis flexed its muscles. Zach Randolph had a monster 20-20 game by scoring 21 points and 21 rebounds. Marc Gasol's 16 points and seven rebounds weren't too shabby either.

Now with a 2-1 lead, the Memphis Grizzlies were again on the verge of upsetting a higher seeded team by winning the whole series. The OKC Thunder had other ideas in mind. In what would be one of the best playoff games in NBA history, the Thunder defeated the Grizzlies in triple overtime 133 to 123. The Thunder capitalized on Memphis' inability to score in the third overtime period. Kevin Durant had 35 points and 13 rebounds. Russell Westbrook made minced meat out of Conley's defense by scoring a career playoff-high 40 points. On the Grizzlies side, the frontline kept them alive by performing monstrously as well. Zach Randolph had 34 points and 16 rebounds while Marc Gasol had a 20-20 of his own by scoring 26 points and grabbing 21 rebounds. It was all for naught in a loss and the series was tied at two wins apiece.

Back in Oklahoma City, the Thunder blew the Grizzlies out with a 27-point win. Memphis obviously had trouble scoring with merely 72 points over four quarters. Marc Gasol had 15 points for the Grizzlies while Durant scored 19 for his team. Home court advantage and the series lead returned to the Thunder with the game five win. The Grizzlies didn't want their season to end just yet when they tied the series 3-3 on a game six victory on their own home floor. Randolph led them with 33 points and 12 rebounds while Gasol struggled to score in double digits.

The series shifted back to Oklahoma for a deciding game seven. This was the first game seven that the Memphis Grizzlies played in the history of the franchise. Despite a hard-fought game, it was the Thunder who prevailed on their home court. The OKC dynamic duo played in top form. Kevin Durant scored at will with 39 points while Russell Westbrook recorded a triple-double, which was only the fifth time in league history that a player recorded such a stat in a game seven. Mike Conley led the Grizzlies with 18 points. Marc only mustered 12 points and 7 boards for the Grizzlies who saw their historic season ending.

Despite bowing out of the playoffs, the Grizzlies showed that they were a very capable team by beating the top-seeded team in the conference and by pushing the OKC Thunder to the limit. Their playoff performance was a testament to how effective the grit-and-grind style was and that Memphis would soon wreak more havoc in the playoffs for years to come.

Despite not having the gaudy numbers that Pau had, Marc was able to reach deeper into the playoffs than his brother ever had while wearing a Grizzlies uniform. It might be because Marc had a better team around him, but it was simply a testament to how good Marc had become. Marc Gasol played his best basketball in the playoffs by averaging 15 points, 11.2 rebounds, 2 assists, and 2 blocks. His playoff statistics were much better than his regular season numbers, and they showed that Marc was a player that a team could count on for a championship run.

All-Star Season

In the offseason prior to the 2011-12 season, the Grizzlies knew that their playoff performance was not a fluke and that their grit-and-grind style was just as effective as any other teams' brand of basketball. First things first, they had to keep their centerpiece on the team. After all, Marc Gasol was their anchor in the middle. Gasol earned a four-year extension from the Grizzlies worth $58 million. Who would have thought that a mere second round draft pick could command such a contract?

The Grizzlies strengthened their bench by adding Marreese Speights, Quincy Pondexter, and Dante Cunningham. The league faced a lockout that shortened training camp and also the regular season to a compressed 65 games. Though the Grizzlies didn't have time to practice their craft due to the shortened training camp, they still played the same grit-and-grind brand of basketball that delivered them to the second round the previous season. They started Tony Allen in place of OJ Mayo who was relegated to a sixth man role. Allen's gritty style of play earned him the nickname "Grindmaster" because he was the Grizzlies' best perimeter defender.

With Allen out in the perimeter and Gasol patrolling the paint, the Grizzlies were the fifth best team in terms of limiting their opponent's scoring. They were also third in the league in opponent's field goal percentage and still led the league in steals. Moreover, their style was perfect for the shortened 65-game season where games were compressed. Their physicality put a toll on opponents and their slow pace kept them fresh throughout the regular season.

Zach Randolph was severely limited in the 2011-12 season because of injuries. He only played 28 games and started only eight of them. This was after his amazing performance in the playoffs the previous year.

Speights picked up the starting role in place of Randolph and he played well enough for a reserve. With Randolph gone for the majority of the regular season, it was Marc Gasol who piled up the inside scoring for the Memphis Grizzlies. Gasol was the second leading scorer in the lineup and was behind only Rudy Gay in that department. He was also their leading rebounder and shot blocker.

It was Marc's presence inside the paint that made the Grizzlies a tough contender for the West. He was obviously the Grizzlies' best player at this point of his career, especially since Zach Randolph was out with an injury. And even if Randolph was available, he did not have the same defensive presence that Marc had. Marc's improved play and his ability to carry the Grizzlies on his back earned him his first ever All-Star selection. Marc Gasol scored four points and grabbed three rebounds in barely 14 minutes in his first All-Star game appearance. The West team went on to win the midseason classic in the strength of All-Star MVP Kevin Durant's 36 points.

By the end of the season, Marc Gasol averaged 14.6 points, 8.9 rebounds, 3.1 dimes, and 1.9 shots blocked. Under his leadership, the Memphis Grizzlies improved their playoffs positioning to the fourth seed with a record of 41 wins and 25 losses. As the fourth seed in the Western Conference, it was the first time in Grizzlies history that they would have home court advantage in the first round. The best news, however, was that Zach Randolph was now healthy for the playoffs and could provide the same type of stellar play he did in the previous playoffs.

The Grizzlies were to go up against the fifth-seeded Los Angeles Clippers led by the duo of superstar point guard Chris Paul and high-flying versatile power forward Blake Griffin. With home court advantage, the Grizzlies did not have to pressure themselves with winning on the road against this much-improved Clippers team.

In a reversal of roles, the Memphis Grizzlies would lose home court advantage with a very tight loss in game one. In fact, the Grizzlies actually led the game in the fourth quarter by as many as 27 points and looked as if they were going to run away with an easy win. However, they were limited to merely one field goal and three points from the 9-minute mark of the fourth because of an intense rally by the Clipper bench. Nick Young led the way for the clippers off the bench with 19 points. For the Grizzlies side, Marc only managed to grab six rebounds while Rudy Gay scored 19. Zach Randolph was nowhere to be found with only six points, which was a far cry back to his game one output in the previous playoffs.

The Grizzlies would bounce back in the second game with a seven-point win. Once again, Marc struggled to find his groove with only 8 points and 7 rebounds. It was once again Rudy Gay who top-scored for the Grizzlies with 21, followed by the 20 points of OJ Mayo coming off the bench, including 10 points in the fourth quarter. Though Chris Paul had 29 points for the Clippers, the team had 21 turnovers forced by the pressure defense of Memphis.

The Los Angeles Clippers would regain the series lead by winning game three when the series shifted over to the Staples Center in LA. It was a tough one-point loss for the Grizzlies who failed to capitalize on the Clippers' missed free throws in the final seconds of the game. The game went down with Rudy Gay cutting down the Clippers lead to one point with two three-pointers. In the end, the Clippers were able to save themselves from a meltdown when they forced Gay to miss a possible game winning shot at the buzzer. Gay had 24 points while Gasol had his first double-double in the series with 11 points and 10 rebounds. Chris Paul led the Clips with 24 points and 11 dimes.

Game four would once again go down to the wire. It was the Clippers that prevailed in overtime with a 101-97 victory in the Staples Center. It was a great point guard battle between Chris Paul and Mike Conley.

Paul scored 27 while Conley had 25. It was Paul's veteran smarts that had them outlasting the Grizzlies. CP3 carried his team in overtime and led the Clippers to a 3-1 series lead over the Grizzlies.

Now on the brink of elimination, the Grizzlies rallied at their home court and won game five by 12 points. Marc Gasol broke out from his scoring slump by registering 23 points. He also had seven rebounds and four assists. Mo Williams off the bench led the Clippers with 20. With a chance of sealing the series at home, the Clippers would again lose to a desperate Grizzlies team in game six. Gasol once again dominated the paint with 23 points for Memphis, who actually trailed by as much as eight points in the fourth quarter. With Marc Gasol finding his scoring touch in their last two wins, the Grizzlies were poised to win the do-or-die game seven back in The Grindhouse.

Despite Gay and Gasol scoring big for the Grizzlies, the other starters nor the bench could muster the energy to help carry the scoring load. The Clippers managed to lead by as much as 10 points in the fourth quarter, and that was all they needed to seal the deal and the series. Once again, the Clippers bench outplayed their Grizzlies counterpart. The Grizzlies managed to score only 72 the entire game despite limiting the Clips to 82. Their defense worked but their offense, especially their bench scoring, stank the entire series.

After a good run in the playoffs the previous year, the Grizzlies were eliminated in the first round this time, even though they had a better seeding. Zach Randolph was obviously not the same version of himself as the previous season. And though they had Rudy Gay back in their lineup for the playoffs, his scoring could not make up for the lack of the Grizzlies' bench production. Marc Gasol had the same scoring numbers he had in the regular season, but he obviously struggled to rebound the ball with only 6.7 rebounds the entire first round.

Defensive Player of the Year Winner

As seen from their first round loss against the Clippers, it was obvious that what the Grizzlies lacked was bench production. Their starters were well balanced. They had wing scoring from Rudy Gay, Conley and Allen provided good ball pressure, and Randolph together with Gasol dominated the paint. However, when the second unit would come in, only OJ Mayo could muster up points from the bench. The rest of their bench unit would often struggle. In order to resolve this issue, they brought in Jerryd Bayless and Wayne Ellington during the offseason to provide bench scoring. They did not decide to bring back OJ Mayo, who was their only scoring punch off the bench. They did not even sign his qualifying offer. The Grizzlies obviously thought Mayo had no place in their team.

Under the defensive leadership of Marc Gasol, the Memphis Grizzlies further improved their defensive capabilities in the 2012-13 NBA season. The Grizzlies became the most dreaded defensive team in the league and all offenses feared them no matter how many scorers they had. Memphis surrendered a league-low average of merely 89.3 points per game during the 2012-13 season. Their opponents could not even attempt as many shots as they wanted to as the Grizzlies also limited the number of field goal attempts per game. They also maintained the consistent ball pressure that they always had by ranking sixth highest in steals per game. Moreover, the slow pace of the game and the presence of their big man in the paint helped them in limiting their opponents to a league-low 39.1 rebounds per game. All of this was made possible by the defensive tandem of Marc Gasol and Tony Allen.

In the middle of the season, the Grizzlies traded away their top scorer Rudy Gay in a six-player, three-team trade. Gay and Haddadi were sent over to the Toronto Raptors while the Grizzlies obtained Ed Davis and Jose Calderon. They immediately shipped Calderon to the Pistons for Tayshaun Prince and Austin Daye. The Rudy Gay trade was a money-saving move on the part of the Grizzlies who wanted to get rid of Gay's massive contract.[xix] Memphis also acquired Jon Leuer in a trade for Speights, Josh Selby, and Ellington.

Gasol, Randolph, and Conley all picked up the scoring pace with the departure of Rudy Gay. Mike Conley, at season's end, had a career high in scoring average with 14.6. A healthier Zach Randolph continued to dominate the paint and the rebounds by averaging a double-double with 15.4 points and 11.2 rebounds. The biggest story of improvement, however, was the defensive presence of Marc Gasol.

Marc Gasol had a scoring differential of +5.4 points. That 5.4-point differential, ranking him second among all league centers. When Marc was on the floor, the Grizzlies had a differential of +7.5. When he was sitting on the bench, the Grizzlies were -3.9. With those numbers, it was evident that Gasol was the defensive anchor of the team. At season's end, Gasol was named the Defensive Player of the Year for the first time in his career. He was also on the All-Defensive Second Team. Those awards were a testament to how Gasol made his team better just by defending the floor. If we flash back to 2007, scouting reports said that Gasol was a defensive liability because of his limited mobility. Gasol had proven them wrong by improving his conditioning and by being one of the smartest defenders in the league. Gasol did not defend by blocking shots. Instead, he did so by rotating optimally on defense and by contesting shots at the rim. In the 2012-13 season, Gasol averaged 14.1 points, 7.8 rebounds, 4 assists (highest among centers), 1 steal, and 1.7 blocks. Marc was also named to the All-NBA Second Team.

The Memphis Grizzlies finished the season with an all-time franchise record of 56 wins and 26 losses. Their record was good enough for the fifth playoff spot in the ultra-competitive Western Conference. If they had played in the East, their record would have earned them a top three spot in the seeding. Nevertheless, the Grizzlies were happy to be back in the postseason for a third consecutive year.

The Grizzlies would face the Los Angeles Clippers once again in the first round. This time, it was a reversal of roles because the Clippers had home court advantage since they were the higher seeded team. The Clips immediately gave the Grizzlies a run for their money in game one after winning by 21 points. Memphis' starting unit struggled to score and it was Jerryd Bayless who top scored for the Grizzlies with 19 off the bench. Marc Gasol only had 16 on 4 of 12 shooting and it was Chris Paul who led the way for LA with 23 points.

The Clippers made the most out of their home court advantage once again by winning game two. This time, it was a tightly contested game that went down the wire. It took a game-winning bank shot from star point guard Chris Paul to beat the Grizzlies by two points. Mike Conley stepped up big for his team with 28 points and Gasol had 17 and 7. Four of the five Memphis starters scored in the double digits. The duo of Paul and Blake Griffin paved the way for a Clippers victory with each of them scoring more than 20 points. With the Grizzlies failing to snag the home court advantage away from the Clippers, they went back home to Memphis, intent on also making the most out of their home court. The Grindhouse was ultra-hostile to the Clippers in game three when they managed to score only 82 points the entire game. Memphis went back to their basic offense, which was to give the ball to their big men and to let them pound their way toward points. Zach Randolph had 27 points and 11 rebounds while Marc Gasol had 16 points and 8 boards on their way to a 12-point victory at home.

Memphis managed to even up the series by winning again at home. This time, it was a 21-point blowout win. Using the same tactic they utilized in the previous game, the Grizzlies' big men went grinding at the interior defense of the Clippers. Gasol and Randolph each had 24 points with 13 and 9 rebounds respectively. Paul and Griffin each had 19 in a losing effort for the Clippers who were unable to hold their own against the size and strength of the Memphis big guys.

The series was tied at two wins apiece and it shifted back to Los Angeles for game five. Chris Paul played like a man on a mission by scoring 35 points. Yet, it was Gasol and Randolph yet again who carved up the Clippers' defense for another double-digit win for the Grizzlies. Randolph was playing as if it were the 2011 playoffs all over again while Gasol continued to dominate his matchup with DeAndre Jordan. Zach scored 25 and grabbed 11 rebounds while Marc had 21 and 8 of his own. The Grizzlies had won three straight and owned the series lead three wins to two. They were one win away from advancing deeper into the second round.

Facing eliminations, one would expect that the Clippers would dish out all that they had to save their season. This was not the case, however. Memphis outscored LA in all of the first three quarters on their way to a 118-105 victory that sealed the Clippers' fate and advanced the Grizzlies into the second round. Zach Randolph once again bullied his way to 23 points. Conley had 23 points of his own, but it was the bench that gave them the extra punch that they needed. Bayless scored 18 while Pondexter had 10. The Memphis Grizzlies have avenged last year's playoff loss to the Clippers with a 4-2 win in the series.

The Memphis Grizzlies were set to go against the top-seeded Oklahoma City Thunder with the league's leading scorer Kevin Durant. The caveat was that OKC was without their ultra-fast starting point guard Russell Westbrook, who suffered a season-ending injury in their first round encounter against the Houston Rockets. With only one transcendent scorer to defend, it looked as if lady luck was on the side of the Memphis Grizzlies.

With home court advantage, Kevin Durant scored seven straight baskets for the OKC Thunder to beat the Memphis Grizzlies 93 to 91. The league's best scorer put up 35 points and collected 15 rebounds. Marc Gasol and Zach Randolph led the way for the Grizzlies once again by scoring 20 and 18 respectively to go along with 10 rebounds each.

Knowing that the Thunder were depleted, the Grizzlies could just leave Durant to do all the scoring while his other teammates could not buy baskets. That was the exact strategy they employed in order to win game two and quite possibly the rest of the series. Durant scored 36 for the Thunder but it was essentially a one-man scoring crew against a balanced effort by the Grizzlies. Marc Gasol had 24, Randolph had 15, and Conley top scored with 26. The only other help that Durant had was the aging Derek Fisher who scored 19. In the end, Memphis won by six to steal home court and to tie the series one win apiece.

It was more of the same when the series shifted over to Memphis. The Grizzlies utilized a balanced attack while leaving Durant trying to score his team to a victory. Kevin Durant had 25 points, but lacked the help he needed to win over the tough defense of the Grizzlies who won 87 to 81. Gasol dominated his match-up in the paint with 20 points and 9 rebounds. Tony Allen and Mike Conley had 14 apiece while Jerry Bayless was big off the bench with 11 points.

Using the same strategy over and over again, the Grizzlies won game four in overtime at their home court despite a strong 17-point start from the OKC Thunder. Randolph and Gasol each had a double-double game. Zach had 23 and 12 while Marc had 23 and 11. Mike Conley had 24 points. Durant sent the game into overtime by hitting a game-tying shot. His Thunder only mustered one field goal in the extra period, though. The Memphis Grizzlies were now up three wins to one and were a win away from reaching the Western Conference finals for the first time in franchise history.

In game five back in Oklahoma, the Grizzlies gave no quarter. While they would leave Kevin Durant alone to score at will in the previous four games, they smothered him in game five. Durant scored 21 points on a poor 5-21 shooting and played all 48 minutes for his team. Randolph came up big again by scoring 28 and grabbing 14 rebounds. Marc only had 10 points but came up big with four shots swatted. Four starters were in double digits for Memphis who played a balance attack again. In the end, the Grizzlies prevailed in the game and in the series by once again winning four straight games. They were headed to the Conference finals for the first time in their history.

The Memphis Grizzlies were to go up against a mighty San Antonio Spurs team that featured great ball movement and player involvement in their offense. The most daunting part of this task was that the Spurs could never forget how the Grizzlies humiliated them two playoffs ago. They were intent on taking revenge against the eighth-seeded team that took them out of the postseason in 2011.

In game one, the Grizzlies could not stop the offensive juggernaut of the Spurs. Moreover, their starters struggled to get points of their own. Randolph merely had two points and could not replicate his performance against the Spurs two seasons before. Marc Gasol had 15 and 7 while Conley scored 14. It was Quincy Pondexter who top scored with 17 off the bench. The Spurs utilized a balanced attack with five players in double digits led by Tony Parker's 20 points.

In game two, the Spurs had a game-high 18-point lead. Going into the fourth quarter, they led by 12 points. They would bid farewell to that lead when the Grizzlies buckled down defensively to force them to miss their last eight shots. The Grizzlies forced overtime but failed to deliver in the extra period. The ageless Tim Duncan together with Tiago Splitter outplayed the daunted Memphis big men. Timmy had

17 points, 9 rebounds, and four blocks while Tiago had 14 points and two blocks. Their counterparts Marc and Zach had 12 and 15 points respectively while grabbing 14 and 18 rebounds. Conley and Bayless top scored for the Grizzlies with 18 each in the 89-93 loss. The Spurs had all starters in the double digits.

If there was a team that could put up four wins despite trailing two games in the series, it was the Memphis Grizzlies. They had the best opportunity to do so when the series shifted to The Grindhouse. Despite the energy of the Memphis crowd, the Grizzlies could not match the decade-long experience that the Spurs' main trio had playing together. Duncan turned back the clock by scoring 24 points, Parker had 26, and Ginobili had 19. The trio combined to score 69 points. Meanwhile, the Grizzlies could not hold on to a strong start in the first quarter and could not buy a basket in the overtime period. Gasol had 16 points and 14 rebounds. Randolph played strong as well with 14 points and 15 rebounds. Conley scored 20 and Bayless had 15. They just could not hold on to their fourth quarter lead and couldn't score in the extra period.

The Grizzlies were down three games going into game four. No team in NBA history has ever come back to win a seven-game series after trailing 0-3. The Grizzlies were not spared from the same fate and could not stop Tony Parker. The Frenchman had 37 points. Marc Gasol led the Grizzlies starters with 14 points. The only person who kept them alive was Quincy Pondexter off the bench with 22. It just seemed as if the Memphis starters lost all hope of coming back from the 0-3 deficit, and they just seemed like they gave up the fight in game four.

After losing in game four, Marc Gasol and the Grizzlies became another statistic in the history of the NBA. They failed to come back from the series deficit. Worse, they could not even win a single game against the San Antonio Spurs who finally avenged their loss back in 2011. After scoring and rebounding at will in the previous two series, Marc struggled against the experience of the San Antonio big guys. Marc led the team in blocking in the playoffs with 2.2. He was second in scoring, rebounding, and assists with 17.2, 8.2, and 3.2 respectively. Ultimately though, he could not lead the Grizzlies to a Finals appearance.

Injury Plagued Season and New Coach

In the offseason following their playoff loss to the Spurs, the Grizzlies front office decided not to renew head coach Lionel Hollins' contract. This was despite Hollins leading the team to three straight playoff appearances and to a trip to the Western Conference finals, their best postseason performance in franchise history. This was despite developing guys like Mike Conley and Marc Gasol, who won Defensive Player of the Year, into borderline All-Star players. Nevertheless, the reason for essentially firing Hollins was a so-called difference in perspectives.[xx]

Assistant Dave Joerger was promoted to the head coaching duty for the Grizzlies. Joerger was also the defensive coordinator for Memphis when Hollins coached the team. Though keeping the core of the team intact, Dave Joerger opted to play at a faster pace than the Grizzlies had played the previous three seasons.[xxi] However, Joerger also planned on maintaining the same kind of defense that made the Grizzlies a highly feared team over the past three years. The Grizzlies bolstered their bench by adding a capable back-up center Kosta Koufous in an offseason trade with the Denver Nuggets. They also signed Mike Miller, who played for the Grizzlies much earlier in his career, for outside shooting (something they lacked) and for leadership. The Grizzlies also picked up big point guard Nick Calathes, who never played in the NBA since getting drafted in 2009, for his defensive toughness. On paper, it seemed as if this Memphis Grizzlies squad would be much stronger than the one that made the Western Conference finals.

The Grizzlies did not start the 2013-14 season the way they wanted to. The team was just starting to adjust to the faster-paced style that Joerger wanted them to play. After all, the team was not built to play quickly due to their lack of athleticism. Despite playing fast, they were still a pretty good defensive team. Under Joerger, the team was still the slowest paced in the league but their defense dropped to 94.6 per game, the third lowest, all the way from barely 90 points last year.

The worst for the year came when Marc Gasol suffered a sprained MCL in his left knee in November during a game against the Spurs. No surgery was needed for his injury, but Marc was sidelined indefinitely.[xxii] He would miss the next two months for the Memphis Grizzlies and the team won only 10 games and lost 13 during the time of Marc's absence. With the Grizzlies struggling during Gasol's injury, anyone would obviously conclude that Marc was the most valuable Grizzly.

The Grizzlies further made offseason moves by trading for Courtney Lee in exchange for Jerryd Bayless. Courtney Lee provided some added scoring in the absence of Marc Gasol. This also allowed Joerger to move Tony Allen over to the bench. Lee would prove to be a valuable shooter and scorer for the Grizzlies, even to this day.

Losing Marc in the middle of the season was a big blow to the Grizzlies, but they still managed to win more than they lost. Coming into the All-Star Weekend, the Grizzlies had a record of 29 wins and 23 losses. Once Marc Gasol came back, the Grizzlies were rolling again. Furthermore, Dave Joerger resorted to going back to the grit-and-grind style that made the Grizzlies a perennial playoff contender the past three years. In the 59 games that Gasol played for Memphis that season, the Grizzlies had 40 wins and only 19 losses. At season's end, Marc Gasol averaged 14.6 points, 7.2 boards, 3.6 assists, and 1.3 blocks while leading the Grizzlies to a 50-32 record that was good enough for seventh in the Western Conference. Zach Randolph and Mike Conley led the team in scoring with 17.4 and 17.2 respectively. It was Gasol's presence in the paint that got them a playoff spot.

The Grizzlies would face the second-seeded Oklahoma City Thunder in the first round of the playoffs. This time, Russell Westbrook was completely healthy and ready to assist that year's Most Valuable Player Kevin Durant in leading the team since he was unable to do so in the last playoffs. OKC would beat the Grizzlies in double digits in game one on the strength of a terrific fourth quarter. Kevin Durant picked up where he left off in the previous season's meeting by scoring at will. He finished the game with 33 points while his partner-in-crime Russell Westbrook had 23 points and 10 rebounds. Oddly enough, the Thunder were the only team to win at home that day. Zach Randolph had a good game with 21 points and 11 rebounds. Marc was solid as well with 16 points in a losing effort.

The Grizzlies had a solid effort in game two by almost winning the game in regulation. Kevin Durant sank in an impossible three-pointer to send the game to overtime. Nevertheless, the Grizzlies buckled up defensively in the extra period to win the game and steal home court advantage. Randolph had another solid game with 25 points. Marc Gasol and Courtney Lee chipped in 16 each while Mike Conley had 19. However, it was Beno Udrih off the bench who was the biggest story of the night by scoring 14 points. Durant was pushed to the limit by Tony Allen, but still managed 36 points. Westbrook scored 29.

When the series shifted over to Memphis for game three, the Grizzlies gained the series lead in a tight finish again in overtime. The Grizzlies came into the fourth quarter with a 10-point lead and actually led by as much as 17 in the final period, but it disappeared after OKC scored 17 unanswered points. Memphis managed to hold on to a three-point win. The Grizzlies bench came out big again. Allen had 16 and Udrih had 12. Conley led four Grizzlies in double digits with 20. Marc Gasol had 14 points and 8 rebounds. Both Durant and Westbrook recorded 30 points.

Memphis led the series 2-1 heading into game four. In what would be the third straight overtime game in the series, OKC would come out victorious despite the Grizzlies limiting the production of the Thunder dynamic duo. KD and Russ only had 15 each, but it was Reggie Jackson off the bench who came saved the game for OKC with 32 points. Jackson also scored the last five points for the Thunder to force the overtime win. Marc Gasol had a double-double with 23 points and 11 rebounds.

The series was now tied two wins apiece and returned to Oklahoma for game five. The Grizzlies and the Thunder made NBA playoff history by playing four straight overtime games. With the Grizzlies leading late in the fourth quarter, the Thunder rallied to force overtime. It was veteran Grizzly Mike Miller who gave the needed boost off the bench. Miller hit five three-pointers in the game including two in the extra period to lead the Grizzlies to a 3-2 lead in the series. Miller finished with 21 points. Randolph and Gasol each had double-doubles with 20-10 and 11-15 points-rebounds respectively.

The Grizzlies were now headed home to The Grindhouse for game six and a possible win to advance to the second round. The Thunder would foil the Grizzlies' hopes by both starting and finishing strong. OKC won the game by 20 points on the strength of Kevin Durant's 36 points after he was criticized for his unreliable play. Russell Westbrook scored 25 to help the Thunder force game seven in their home court. Gasol led the Grizzlies with 17 points.

Memphis opened game seven on the road strongly by scoring 36 points in the first quarter and leading by nine coming into the second despite Zach Randolph being suspended for a scuffle in game six. However, OKC would rally back in the second quarter to lead the game by three coming into the second half. The Thunder held on to their lead until the end of the game. The OKC Thunder duo combined for 60 points and Russell Westbrook became only the second player to have two game seven triple-doubles. Marc Gasol had 24 points but struggled to get rebounds. The whole team managed to rebound only 29 points the whole game.

With OKC winning game seven, the Memphis Grizzlies faced their second first round exit in four years. Even though the Grizzlies lost, they won three out of the four overtime games in the series and forced the much-higher seeded Thunder team to seven games. Had they had home court advantage, things would have been different. Had Marc Gasol been healthy the entire regular season, the Grizzlies would have had home court advantage in the first round.

Return to All-Star Form and Becoming One of the NBA's Best Centers

Dave Joerger finally figured out that the identity of the Grizzlies was that they were a slow-paced grit-and-grind team. Joerger did not force them to play faster, but returned to how they were playing during the time of Hollins. The Grizzlies kept the core intact but added several pieces. They signed veteran and former All-Star Vince Carter in the offseason. They had long wanted Carter added to the team to supplement the scoring left by Gay. It was only in the offseason prior to the 2014-15 season that they were able to get him in Grizzlies uniform.

In the middle of the season, the Grizzlies made a move to add more scoring to the team. The team moved Tayshaun Prince and Russ Smith to make way for Jeff Green from the Boston Celtics.[xxiii] Prince was an aging player and was not the defender he used to be. With Jeff Green on the roster, the Grizzlies now had the wing scoring they'd been missing since trading away Rudy Gay two seasons ago. Green would often be relegated to the bench as a sixth man, but would sometimes start games.

In the 2014-15 season, Marc Gasol was not only the best player on his team, he was also the best scorer. Gasol was the focal point on both offense and defense.

He would score at the post and also make plays for his teammates at the center position. On defense, he maintained the same ability to rotate that made him Defensive Player of the Year two seasons previously. Marc Gasol credits this increased production on both ends to his improved conditioning. In the offseason, Marc worked on improving his physique by working on a vegetarian diet.[xxiv] By season's opener, he looked leaner and more muscular than he has ever been in his whole career and he actually lost 15 pounds.

With Marc Gasol leading the way for the Grizzlies, the team had the best record early in the season and went 15 wins and only two losses by the end of November. With his increased production and with the performance of the Grizzlies, Marc was a strong contender in the conversation for MVP for the first time in his career. Marc Gasol would be named as an All-Star for the second time since 2012. More importantly, Marc was a starter for the Western Conference All-Stars.

In the 2015 All-Star game, Marc Gasol would make history with his brother Pau. Marc and Pau would become only the first brothers in the NBA to start and play against each other on opposing All-Star teams. Pau started for the Eastern Conference team with his rejuvenated play with the Chicago Bulls. The Gasol brothers would play well in the midseason classic. Pau had 10 points and 12 rebounds while Marc had 6 points and 10 rebounds to help the Western All-Stars win over the East. Russell Westbrook stole the show by scoring 41 points off the bench to win All-Star MVP honors.

At season's end, Marc Gasol averaged 17.4 points, 7.8 rebounds, 3.8 dimes, and 1.6 blocks. He was named to the All-NBA First Team and was widely considered as the best center in the NBA together with Dwight Howard and DeMarcus Cousins. Marc's numbers did not support that claim but his skill set, passing ability, and his defensive presence were what made him the best at his position. Marc's leadership allowed the

Grizzlies to finish the season with a 55-27 win-loss record, placing them as the fifth seed in the West. The Grizzlies returned to being the most dreaded defense in the league, but they were still capable enough to score a lot of points.

In the first round of the 2015 playoffs, the Grizzlies squared off with the Portland Trailblazers led by dynamic point guard Damian Lillard and versatile power forward LaMarcus Aldridge. The Grizzlies quickly stole home court advantage in game one, a game they never trailed from start to finish. They won by 14 points with both Gasol and Randolph having double-doubles. Beno Udrih added some scoring punch from the bench with 20 points. Aldridge had 32 for the Blazers. The Grizzlies stole home court advantage and started with an early series lead.

Game two was just as easy for the Grizzlies. They won the game 97-82. Lee and Conley led the game with 14 each and Gasol played good defense throughout the game to limit every other Blazer except LaMarcus

Aldridge who scored 24. The Grizzlies quickly jumped to a 2-0 series lead heading over to their home court in Memphis.

The Grizzlies, however, suffered an important loss. They lost Mike Conley due to facial fractures when he collided with Portland's CJ McCollum. Nevertheless, the Grizzlies jumped to an insurmountable 3-0 lead over the Trailblazers on the strength of Marc Gasol's 25 points. Nick Calathes scored 13 while filling in for the injured Conley. Courtney Lee also chipped in 20 points. For the Blazers, four players scored more than 20 points led by Nicolas Batum's 27. The Grizzlies were only one win away from the second round. They were virtually already locked in to advance to the next phase because no team has ever come back from a 3-0 deficit in a seven-game series.

The Portland Trailblazers still breathed life into the team when they managed to avoid elimination in game five. The Blazers started the first half strong but faltered in the third quarter. However, they staved off the Grizzlies with a strong fourth quarter. Damian Lillard came out big for his team by scoring 32 points. For the Grizzlies, Marc Gasol top scored with 21 points, 7 rebounds, and 6 assists. This was all the Blazers had to offer in their playoff appearance.

The Memphis Grizzlies formally advanced to the second round after defeating the Portland Trailblazers in game five 99-93. They did not waste time nor miss a second from start to finish to try to eliminate the Blazers. The Grizzlies frontline flexed their muscles on the inside. Marc Gasol top scored and top rebounded with 26 and 14 respectively. Zach Randolph had 16 points and 8 rebounds. Despite losing Mike Conley in the last two games, the Grizzlies were still strong enough to get rid of the Blazers.

The Memphis Grizzlies would proceed to the second round and face the surprising top-seeded team Golden State Warriors. The Warriors had a historic 67-15 regular season and were led by the 2015 Most Valuable Player Stephen Curry together with his "splash brother" Klay Thompson. Despite facing the best team in the NBA that season, the Grizzlies would take the fight to the Golden State Warriors.

In game one of the Western Conference semi-finals, the Warriors easily handled the Grizzlies in a 101-86 victory. Curry led the way for the Warriors with 22 points. Gasol and Randolph dominated their match-up in the paint in a losing effort. Marc had 21 while Zach had 20.

The Grizzlies quickly bounced back in game two to effectively steal home court advantage. The highlight of the game was the return of Mike Conley from his facial fractures. Conley would wear a mask for the entire game, but it did not hinder him in the very least. In 27 minutes, he scored 22 points to win his matchup with the MVP. Four of the Memphis starters scored in double digits. Curry led the Warriors with 19 points on a bad shooting night.

With home court advantage in their hands, the Grizzlies went home to The Grindhouse to try to take an insurmountable command over the series. Going back to their basics, Marc Gasol and Zach Randolph dominated the paint yet again. Gasol had 21 points and 15 rebounds before fouling out. Randolph chipped in 22 points and 8 rebounds. Conley and Lee had 11 each. Curry and Klay Thompson scored more than 20 each for the reeling Warriors.

The Grizzlies now had command over the series with a 2-1 lead over the Warriors and were looking to increase their series control. The Warriors had other things in mind. Golden State both started and ended strong to rout the Grizzlies on their own home floor 101 to 84. Curry exploded with 33 points. Marc Gasol led the Grizzlies with yet another double-double. He had 19 points, 10 rebounds, and 6 assists. The series was now tied 2-2 and was headed back to the Bay Area for game five.

The Warriors yet again stayed consistent the entire game from the first period up to the end of the game to blow the Grizzlies out 98 to 78. Klay Thompson led the Warriors with 21 points while Curry had 18 points all on three-pointers. Marc Gasol and Zach Randolph were the lone bright spots for the Grizzlies with double-double each. Gasol had 18 and 12. Randolph had 13 and 10. As quick as that, the Warriors now had the series lead 3-2 and the Grizzlies were one loss away from bowing out of the playoffs yet again.

The Grizzlies had a chance to force the series to a deciding game seven. They were back at their home floor, The Grindhouse. The Grizzlies needed to buckle down on their defense harder to stop the reigning MVP from scoring at will. However, nothing they did to defend Curry worked. Steph Curry torched them with 32 points and he hit eight three-pointers. Meanwhile, Gasol had 21 points and 15 rebounds but his effort was for naught. The Grizzlies were unable to break the Warriors offense and could not force a seventh game.

Despite Marc playing at the highest level he has ever played in his career, the Grizzlies did not have enough in them to reach the Finals to have a chance of winning an NBA championship. Marc averaged 18.8 points, 9.8 rebounds, 4.2 assists, and 1.6 blocks during the playoffs. Those were his best numbers ever in both the regular season and the postseason. Even though the Grizzlies lost the series to the Warriors, a lot of experts have speculated that if Conley had been one hundred percent healthy the entire series, they could have won. In the end, the Warriors went on the Finals to win it all. In the offseason following the loss to the Warriors, Marc Gasol became one of the biggest free agents in the NBA, both figuratively and literally. Many teams would have wanted to sign the 7'1" 30-year old All-Star. In the end, Marc Gasol stayed with the team and in the place he has called home ever since he came in as an overweight high school kid from Barcelona, Spain in 2002. Marc signed a $110 million five-year contract to remain in Grizzlies uniform.[xxv]

The Memphis Grizzlies maintained their core and their style of play coming into the 2015-16 NBA season. One of their best offseason acquisitions was hard-nosed defender Matt Barnes. The addition of Barnes allowed the Grizzlies to start him on the wing and to relocate Lee and Green to the bench for some second unit scoring. The Grizzlies also added Mario Chalmers in exchange for Beno Udrih in a season trade with the Miami Heat. Chalmers has become one of the most important players off the bench for the Grizzlies since coming over. Another player that has been playing well is JaMychal Green who filled in for the often injured Zach Randolph.

Currently, Marc Gasol has maintained the same type of All-Star caliber of play to start the season. In 21 games, Marc Gasol has averaged 16.3 points, 7.7 rebounds, 3.8 assists, and 1.2 blocks. After starting the season slowly, his Memphis Grizzlies are sitting at a 12-9 record and are the fourth best team in the West.

Chapter 5: Marc Gasol's Personal Life

Marc Gasol was born in Barcelona Spain on January 29, 1985. He is currently 30 years old. His parents Augusti and Marisa both played basketball in the past. Augusti worked as a hospital administrator while Marisa was a doctor. Both have since relocated with their children to Memphis.

Marc has two other brothers. Pau Gasol is the eldest among the Gasol brothers. He stands at 7 feet tall and has played for the Memphis Grizzlies, the Los Angeles Lakers, and currently for the Chicago Bulls. Pau is a Rookie of the Year winner, a five-time All-Star, and a two-time NBA Champion, both times with the Lakers. Marc's younger brother Adria was supposed to play at UCLA in college, but never saw minutes. He stands at 6'10" and is the shortest among the Gasol siblings. He plays professional basketball in Spain and has played for CB Santfeliuenc in 2012-13 and currently plays for CB La Palma since 2014.

Marc Gasol is currently married to Cristina Blesa. They have been together since 2006 and have been married since July 7, 2013. Cristina is merely 5'9" compared to the 7'1" Marc Gasol. Together, they have a daughter named Julia who was born in September 2014. Cristina was one of the focal points in Marc's career as she helped him eat healthy and lose weight. The couple currently resides in Memphis, Tennessee.

Marc runs the Gasol Foundation together with Pau. The Gasol Foundation aims to help young people live healthier lives through sports, proper nutrition, guidance, and counseling. The foundation runs both in the United States and in the Gasol's home country of Spain.

Chapter 6: Marc Gasol's Legacy and Future

players, but also as one of the best centers of all time. Standing at 7'1" and weighing in at almost 270 lbs., Marc is a giant center. Despite his size, Marc moves with grace on the basketball court and has the same kind of footwork that his brother Pau has always had. Marc has a sweet shooting touch that no other center in the league has. Though Marc can swish the ball all the way out to the three-point line, he rarely does so and mostly takes those shots within the perimeter. Gasol is also the best passing center in the league right now and is actually the second best assist man in the Grizzlies lineup. He can see over the defense and always makes the correct passes. Off the ball, Gasol is both a roller and a popper on screen situations. He can catch the ball with ease after a hard screen to roll to the basket or to spot up to shoot perimeter jumpers. With all those things in mind, Marc's combination of size, grace, shooting, and passing makes him one of the most unique centers in the history of the NBA.

Defensively, Marc is up there with the likes of Dwight Howard, Tyson Chandler, and Joachim Noah as the top defending centers. Like Chandler, Marc does not block a lot of shots but can alter a lot of them. Marc's best feature as a defender is his ability to read pick and roll situations, a skill that is a rarity in centers. He can easily rotate to the open man whenever there is a breakdown in defense and he usually finds a way to clog up the paint no matter how well the opposing team performs plays.

With Marc Gasol's unique skill set, the center position has changed a lot in terms of purpose. Now, a lot of centers have been the focal point in running an offense. Guys like Joachim Noah, Andrew Bogut, and Pau Gasol can all run an offense at the post whenever they play center. Also, many centers now dwell out of the paint to shoot jump shots or set up their teammates. Marc has become a pioneer in that kind of a movement for centers. Probably in a matter of years, we may see a new kind of center called the "point center" because of how Marc has paved the way for playmaking centers that can pass and shoot. With how the NBA has become a point guard league, centers that play big inside the paint have become a rarity. Even though Marc Gasol is not your conventional center, you can still ask him to play the role of the giant center because of his size and his ability to post-up in the paint.

Marc Gasol has also become one of the best Spanish basketball players in history alongside his brother Pau and fellow Spaniard Ricky Rubio. They have turned Spain into arguably the second best basketball country in the world. He has helped Spain win two gold medals in the FIBA European Cup, a gold medal in the FIBA World Championships, and two silver medals in the Olympics. For the Spanish National Basketball Team, Marc has averaged 9.5 points and 5.3 rebounds ever since he donned the country's colors back in 2006. When all is said and done, Marc Gasol will probably be the best Spanish basketball player in history next to Pau Gasol.

Marc Gasol has arguably been the Memphis Grizzlies' franchise player since coming over to the NBA in 2008. His numbers don't always show it, but he has always been their best and most important player on the court, even though he doesn't score or rebound as much as his other teammates do. The proof of that is how much better the Grizzlies are when he is healthy and on the floor because Marc is the personification of the Grizzly's grit-and-grind style due to his defensive presence in the paint. He does not block a lot of shots, but has become a Defensive Player of the Year winner because of how well he rotates on defense and because of how well he reads the offensive sets of each opponent on the fly.

Marc is neither the best scorer nor the best rebounder in Grizzlies history. Those accolades belong to his older brother Pau. Nevertheless, Marc is the best player in Grizzlies history not because of his numbers but because of how he has brought the Grizzlies out of limbo and turned them into a perennial playoff contender. He has brought the Memphis Grizzlies deeper into the playoffs than any other Grizzlies player in the past. Marc currently holds second place in terms of games played for the Grizzlies with 538. He is also second in total minutes played. True to his role as the main defender, Marc is the best defensive rebounder in Grizzlies history with a total of 3135 rebounds and is second in total blocks. And though he has yet to win championships like his brother Pau, his current stellar pace of play might be good enough to help his team contend for a title in the next few seasons.

With how Marc is locked up with Memphis for the next five years or so and with how the team's front office is intent on playing the grit-and-grind style, it is not farfetched to say that Marc will continue to be the best and most important player on the Grizzlies' lineup for years to come. And with Marc's frontcourt partner Zach Randolph currently facing the effects of father time, Marc will surely be asked to shoulder most of the inside scoring as Randolph continues to diminish with age. As a mentor, Gasol can instill his defensive knowledge into younger big men in the Grizzlies lineup such as JaMychal Green and Brendan Wright, who he faced several times in high school. With Marc's tutelage, Green has become a good young piece for the Grizzlies and has grown to become a floor-stretching big man. Wright, when healthy, has also become a very good defender. With how he has helped the Grizzlies and with how he continues to be the team's most prized possession, Marc will not only be the best player in Grizzlies' uniform for several more years, but he will also continue to be one of the league's best and most complete centers with how he works harder on his conditioning and on improving his ever-growing game.

Final Word/About the Author

I was born and raised in Norwalk, Connecticut. Growing up, I could often be found spending many nights watching basketball, soccer, and football matches with my father in the family living room. I love sports and everything that sports can embody. I believe that sports are one of most genuine forms of competition, heart, and determination. I write my works to learn more about influential athletes in the hopes that from my writing, you the reader can walk away inspired to put in an equal if not greater amount of hard work and perseverance to pursue your goals. If you enjoyed *Marc Gasol: The Inspiring Story of One of Basketball's Most Dominant Centers,* please leave a review! Also, you can read more of my works on *J.J. Watt, Colin Kaepernick, Aaron Rodgers, Peyton Manning, Tom Brady, Russell Wilson, Michael Jordan, LeBron James, Kyrie Irving, Klay Thompson, Stephen Curry, Kevin Durant, Russell Westbrook, Anthony*

Davis, Chris Paul, Blake Griffin, Kobe Bryant, Joakim Noah, Scottie Pippen, Carmelo Anthony, Kevin Love, Grant Hill, Tracy McGrady, Vince Carter, Patrick Ewing, Karl Malone, Tony Parker, Allen Iverson, Hakeem Olajuwon, Reggie Miller, Michael Carter-Williams, John Wall, James Harden, Tim Duncan, Steve Nash LaMarcus Aldridge, Derrick Rose, Paul George, Pau Gasol, and *Kevin* Garnett, in the Kindle Store. If you love basketball, check out my website at claytongeoffreys.com to join my exclusive list where I let you know about my latest books and give you lots of goodies.

Like what you read? Please leave a review!

I write because I love sharing the stories of influential people like Marc Gasol with fantastic readers like you. My readers inspire me to write more so please do not hesitate to let me know what you thought by leaving a review! If you love books on life, basketball, or productivity, check out my website at claytongeoffreys.com to join my exclusive list where I let you know about my latest books. Aside from being the first to hear about my latest releases, you can also download a free copy of *33 Life Lessons: Success Principles, Career Advice & Habits of Successful People*. See you there!

Clayton

References

[i] "About Gasol Foundation". *Gasol Foundation.* Web
[ii] Carchia, E. "Adria Gasol leaves UCLA, Returns to Spain". *Sportando.* 21 August 2013. Web
[iii] "Pau Gasol Biography". *Jock Bio.* Web
[iv] Beck, Howard. "Memphis' Main Man: How Big Macs, Blues City Made Marc Gasol NBA's Top Center". *Bleacher Report.* 13 February 2015. Web
[v] Beck, Howard. "Memphis' Main Man: How Big Macs, Blues City Made Marc Gasol NBA's Top Center". *Bleacher Report.* 13 February 2015. Web
[vi] Beck, Howard. "Memphis' Main Man: How Big Macs, Blues City Made Marc Gasol NBA's Top Center". *Bleacher Report.* 13 February 2015. Web
[vii] Beck, Howard. "Memphis' Main Man: How Big Macs, Blues City Made Marc Gasol NBA's Top Center". *Bleacher Report.* 13 February 2015. Web
[viii] Asaad, Jonathan. "Memphis Grizzlies: A Glimpse of Marc Gasol". *Hoops Habit.* Web
[ix] Beck, Howard. "Memphis' Main Man: How Big Macs, Blues City Made Marc Gasol NBA's Top Center". *Bleacher Report.* 13 February 2015. Web
[x] Beck, Howard. "Memphis' Main Man: How Big Macs, Blues City Made Marc Gasol NBA's Top Center". *Bleacher Report.* 13 February 2015. Web
[xi] Cacciola, Scott. "Marc Gasol Left Memphis as Enigma and Returned as Star". *New York Times.* 11 May 2013. Web
[xii] Beck, Howard. "Memphis' Main Man: How Big Macs, Blues City Made Marc Gasol NBA's Top Center". *Bleacher Report.* 13 February 2015. Web
[xiii] Cacciola, Scott. "Marc Gasol Left Memphis as Enigma and Returned as Star". *New York Times.* 11 May 2013. Web
[xiv] Beck, Howard. "Memphis' Main Man: How Big Macs, Blues City Made Marc Gasol NBA's Top Center". *Bleacher Report.* 13 February 2015. Web
[xv] "Marc Gasol". *NBADraft.net.* Web
[xvi] "Marc Gasol". *Draft Express.* Web
[xvii] "Marc Gasol". *NBADraft.net.* Web
[xviii] Beck, Howard. "Memphis' Main Man: How Big Macs, Blues City Made Marc Gasol NBA's Top Center". *Bleacher Report.* 13 February 2015. Web
[xix] "Rudy Gay Traded to Raptors". *ESPN.* 31 January 2013. Web
[xx] "Lionel Hollins, Grizzlies Part Ways". *ESPN.* 13 June 2013. Web
[xxi] "Griz Make Dave Joerger New Coach". *ESPN.* 28 June 2013. Web
[xxii] Golliver, Ben. "Grizzlies' Marc Gasol Out Indefinitely with MCL Sprain

in Left Knee". *Sports Illustrated.* 23 Nov 2013. Web

[xxiii] "Memphis Grizzlies acquire Jeff Green and Russ Smith in three-team trade with Boston Celtics and New Orleans Pelicans". *NBA.* 2015. Web

[xxiv] Manfred, Tony. "Marc Gasol Lost A Ton Of Weight With A Vegetarian Diet Before Becoming The Biggest Free Agent In The NBA". *Business Insider.* 1 December 2014. Web

[xxv] Wojnarowski, Adrian. "Marc Gasol Agrees to $110 Million Deal With the Grizzlies". *Yahoo Sports.* 6 July 2015. Web

Made in the USA
San Bernardino, CA
11 April 2016